HUMAN TISSUE

ALSO BY WEYMAN CHAN

POETRY

Noise from the Laundry (2008)
Hypoderm (2010)
Chinese Blue (2012)

Published by Talonbooks

HUMAN TISSUE

– a primer for Not Knowing –

Weyman Chan

– poems –

TALONBOOKS

Talonbooks
278 East First Avenue, Vancouver, British Columbia, Canada V5T 1A6
www.talonbooks.com

First printing: 2016

Typeset in Albertan
Printed and bound in Canada on 100% post-consumer recycled paper

Interior design by Typesmith
Cover design by Spencer Williams

Talonbooks acknowledges the financial support of the Canada Council for the Arts, the Government of Canada through the Canada Book Fund, and the Province of British Columbia through the British Columbia Arts Council and the Book Publishing Tax Credit.

LIBRARY AND ARCHIVES CANADA CATALOGUING IN PUBLICATION

Chan, Weyman, author
Human tissue : a primer for not knowing : poems / Weyman Chan.

ISBN 978-0-88922-981-5 (PAPERBACK)

I. Title.

PS8555.H39246H85 2016   C811'.6   C2016-901725-7

for Karl and Christy Siegler

CONTENTS

HUMAN TISSUE

Although we took the fervent yet fleeting life of a mayfly as our model of life, from the dawn to the nuptial flight of this short-lived creature we also reclaimed its treasure of inner life. We still wanted duration to be a profound and immediate richness of being.

—GASTON BACHELARD
Intuition of the Instant

There are two forces: fate and human effort ... bound by these, there is nothing else.

—MAHABHARATA
Book of the Sleeping Warriors

1

SOURCE CODE

REMEDY FOR EVIL AND ITS DAILY CALIBRATION

Ready-or-not from the mountaintop
Uncle Phil points. Far up
a cloudless fish tail
maybe trout
dipped in claws

> the sun's red eye
> following them
> as if both were broken

by religious drops,
wet trout as
ceiling prism. Like any
visual hook, I wasn't safe,
last glance down

> fearful for how we spin
> disaster with doe-eyed
> chance.

Years later I paint
that kestrel white, her exiled lunch
weighed for a feather.
Do all poems end with
catch and release

> to some fishy landing? Water?
> Fire? If some in-between
> slope, I'll cast the mean adrift.

SELLING LITTLE BROTHER

1

Ethical worlds like eighth notes
cut off   dial tone
child missing   your pet bird carries
one lost spirit   the nape of your brother spared.

2

Drive out
the nurse who bathes you because   outside
the seniors home   rivers meet hippocampic quick, quick,
slow

Dial your family not pecking magpies playing dropsy
or dysentery/hepialus/epincytis with any variety
of schistosome among those red clay rice fields
        you stake an unbroken claim to

3

Pretend the dark   has a name
    eyes   kicked off to one side
    riverless belly squeal   ambush
            famine every night you dreamt him
                    wasn't that also pretend

4

Dial red furrow   tall grasses in *Heng Ha* hide
Where's MaMa?   passing grave markers
too thin to cry he lets his hand be led away by the buyer
you   wouldn't mind following them out   of hunger either
nice travelling couple not from around here
hiding their gold teeth to get the best deal if asked
        bitter   water   walk
        forget-me-not   where's MaMa

5

osmanthus esculent
oriole
born to fly away from

every tree leaf stripped bare for food but here
bran muffin chased with prune juice   what if

(nurse desertion)
          by Japanese bayonet
he came running back to you
care to un-starve a ghost?
             your favourite

can't complete the call as dialled please hang up
                after
      selling him   home
    boy and ghost collapse in MaMa's arms

LE MOT JUSTE, or, AUTUMN OF THE PATRIARCH

First thing you told yourself seems
now to be an omen. It happened
to someone outside your own skin.
The zodiac hum of who you were
snaps back like a propeller bowtie.
What discrete assurances used to
slick back your cue, and revel in
those chiming homonyms from
childhood, where "mouth," "head"
(*how, how*) lost their twinning? Or,
they got bumped by "cool," "zero"
(*leng, leng*), or "crazy," "bite" (*ngao,
ngao*), me bagging groceries and
worried I might not understand. So
they'd say, *hao doi*, good boy, as
any harsh undertone might undo
the ascent of my assent. A heart
emoticon for Hello Kitty clocks, Hop
Sing as Mickey Rooney, a Maoist
bird purge every five years. *Jung*
means middle, means growth, but
Sino-cool never made a big dent.
Fashion tired you with its rice grains.
Minnie Riperton's swan falsetto lit
an entire pond of outings down the
fresh aisle. Chess club next, if only to
fit in ... which broke up your late sight
lines like a Matisse. You scrubbed out
stains, black suburb hair, wide nose,

brown eyes softening caution in love.
How now does orientalism flower? Or,
when today's words don't satisfy an
object's belonging? Foreground the
burden. Back then, my eyes resisted
the riddle itself, for a mirror among
humble causes. Nor do I wish to un-
pack colour from culture, much. It
exhausts frivolity. These days it may
be easier to simply hide your face
and let the poem stick out like a sore tongue.

TRANSLATION OF THE FEMININE IN MOVING TIME
for the CBC

The word and the thing dictate the machine and its mind, i.e.,
response, in hopes of applying standard auto-correction, i.e.,
first aid,

              or, witnessing what
              never happened will be suspect.

There's external verifiers like witnesses, though radio sound rooms
have no spycam for edgy denim cockwalkers who
stroll kabuki-like through news excellence.
                    On air
pundits can blur "the mute facticity of the feminine" (Butler) –

as it applies to faith recordings – what we're talking about should
apply as well to those shot while eating.
Or in the last seconds sipping tea. One
          can't assume the one in the bomb vest liked it rough.

Now there *are* conventions: more and more talkers
asking
what happened.
A teddy bear might be asked to turn away.
The elephant in the sound room, asked not to play earworm to
                 one's cult of charm, might
                 ponder
                 higher concerns.

KIDS' GEOMETRY

Little lost boy, you'd nothing to say to the officer
the world a detached aerial
of justice spreading its dead perfumes

when to impress some friends your
brother lobbed a rock that smashed your knee
so you'd stop following

but there was no one to cry to when you got home
so you sat down and spotted a roll of twine
walked it like a mythic thread back to the crime scene

across two city streets the twine travels
until a cop cruiser slams the brakes and
his unloved uniform approaches

he rejects sorrow so you stop crying
and forgive when he tells you to wind up the twine
though for a sublime second you say no

you can't take back time

HERE YOU ARE LOOKING AT THE STARS AGAIN

Light. Fallen from its source.
Kinship, anchoring my own shadow
to that twinkle of helium and
hydrogen-iced Perseids

so far it must pierce the sky
(no lullaby)
to reach my seeing into.

Stepmom sighed, *Na ngit-hou sai.*
Clear joy in the sun's heat
on her neck, turned from us. The sun
broke away from memory. And she, from us,

might not have wondered why the sun
fails, carving blind to divide night
from day-shadow and back pain,
skulking the bottom inch of death

where we sleep, half
firmament, half grove. Wait
for morning's
whim: her cradle, my cave.

2

FOREIGN PROTOTYPE

PARABLES FOR FRANKENSTEIN

1

Any scream but his.
Hound screed,
        'swounds!
               Harquebusery?

Half kitten half Whatsit,
        scavenged
               precioushead   haruspicy
if and when
        they gut him.

Wolves: fourteen times. Bears: twice.
               With his bare hands.

Snow. Rain. Lay with skunks, cretin,
    hunchback   mute cunctation

              shed
           your jigsaw carrion.

2

Pileated. Ridged. Whooping.   Symbiont spotted
           hidden   or mimicked

              Aiiiiii emmmmm — his infortuned first utterance.

Clowns and fire-eaters. Motley intermittence and their repute.
Like birds we hid. Fantastic hoops of fabric, paper and fire, this
audience-pleaser hails *presto!* under the loopy stripes of the big top.
              As for sweet things —

that first dear flower held out by the lumberjack's daughter, he
held too dearly. Her not-waking-up also brought her father to an
end. It was then he understood that without speech, without a
way to explain moods, he might as well CRY.
              Disappear in someone else's movie.

3

Goatwoman's cabin. Speak to a door and it opens. She smelt fugitive
before, cloistered him to help feed the fire. Fetch water, cultivate her bed.
Words useless at first. Grunt-grass of sweat, mixed with horse.
Skin on skin. Soon, no hunger surprises either of them.

1. Astronomy teaches us duration of sensation.

2. The cave no longer surrounds, but you're still a cave away
   from what you see.

3. AQP4 tetramer channels in astrocyte feet can swell
   those wide refugee hips –

4. my buckcherry valentine

5. death would be a velvet equivocation for all concerned

6.

] even pity rewards its exception [

3.1

Odin traded one eye for deeper knowledge. Faust sold his soul.

A century passes. Because he liked sweet things, he's in Marple Bridge, delivering Coca-Cola from a night truck where no one looks at him. Next to the grocery store is a man who looks at him. Sweet Caps are flared, SNIGGERING EYEFULS exchanged. Back to Turing's place. Long-distance runner, hard kisser, given to sketching shapes in air when possessed. The man breathes numbers.

Later Turing shares his newest equations. Structured proofs haunt each line in space. Values spill their seed like forms of argument crying under a rock, seizing permutation, while Turing, wrapped in those lunken arms, chases contact-dependency. Diffusion-driven inhibition. Explains how morphogenic potency lurches forward to seed the next. And the next. Phyllotactic leopard spots, cowrie stripes. Biometric sightlines.

The first reading rainbow was a functional disaster. Now, nature's ribosomes chomp down on code, spewing being from nonsense.

Chemically castrated, cast away from Bletchley, a hermit to formulae that can't explain *centre* to a goddamn daisy, Turing reaches out to him with the name —
Lurch — a sudden birth. Delivered to his door.

3.2

Years later, cities. Bright epidemics. Lurch craves dark corners,
becoming photogenic at night. Always around Halloween, so he
could be unveiled and admired ... sort of.
Equal to his lack — clacked jaw, gutturally spluttered *f*'s and
v's. Cement and glass, to cage his wild particles. Stoke the fire,
shovel out surfaces. Under what failed subsistence do shadows
contend? Old growth allows wolves. So it is with wishing
monsters, disappeared on account of *if*. If —
He quotes Milton, finds Whitman in a word search, plays
Balderdash. Now who's-the-cleverest tooler of meme gags?
Capers slip between badly stitched lips — his cricoid bulge-eyed
by our host. She seats him at the baby grand, and within minutes,
Clair de Lune floats among the sculptures.

Oh, happy, happy innocence!
Dictionary cut-ups will assess the misfit. *A fulsome man is but
erthe and claye*. Without wit, the unironed and untoward have
crept into our radial piping, thus shit from porcelain, one lump
or two, whose babes suck and cry to synthpop.

Halston. Bleu de Chanel. C.K.
Colognes trafficking *feel*.

3.54

This pain leaves no visible mark.

In one version, Ms. Shelley devalues kinship in word made flesh
~~whose soul she aborts:~~
... no name to give this black angel of my making.

Another version floats Lurch out into the world stripped of
ancestral pedigree, and this note:
Koi-ga yeh-chu ngeen, mee-tueh do-muht. Kwei muht-ah hek-uhk.
This cave man, I don't know what he's about. He'll eat anything.

Charades help him speak. Plosive word-sounds, !Kung tongue-
clicks smacking fruit off the limb. Whichever family burdened
itself with him was destroyed.

Some used him for his body. A room full of avuncular voyeurs,
gophers, self-proclaimed Nosferati and ruined angels in mid-
congress, seemed noisy for all the wrong reasons, thought
Lurch, retreating after the deed.

How apropos that freaks like him, cut off from the whys and
wherefores of their origin, end up as bedtime bogeymen,
bungled monsters fenced by moral chagrin.

4.7

Planet of dark wounds —
dove on rock renders what I rue with the same ardour my mother
employed in quitting me. (1829)

Counts on both hands the number of times he's been driven out.
By torch, lamp, flashlight, hounds:

Stay lonely, with no soul to trade, other than this birth defect, this
thirst for knowledge (1890)

an applause apparatus   (eyelids bared, epineurally sewn)

Body gone sour —
I passed a stone, before the witching hour —
must death court me, as a bee to her flower? (1820)

From a place unwritten, molten streets freshen the lower east
side. An old herbalist appears from the back room of his keep.
He has no eyes. I take the man's hands. Place them on my scars.
The herbalist nods, turns to measure pinches and handfuls of
dried twisted greys and browns. Drink this. Boil and immerse
your hands and face into that. A child's voice, issuing from the
heavens it would seem, translates her grandfather's voice. (1969)

4

Cell prep on a fish hook, who made thee?
· celibate devilry the closest knowledge
· gelled from vitreous rumour
· 1 assessment jig and 2 mental ovaries
· ephemeral self-interest, mitigated by an uncivil modus vivendi
· from whom
· you speak

towards [edit] Fibroblast Growth Factor 18 variant truncations beyond
the signal peptide domain of the N-terminus, which activate FGFR3
with increased specificity (U.S. Patent # 9,226,949, Yayon et al.) of
employee satisfaction

one bee's target coition
ultraviolet landing strips crowd the bosom

or do hyaline cues sex mate-anxiety to kill the darling in your head?

5

He peers.

6

She assesses to crave.

7

1. Research description re: docile vs. invasive hive minds

The sound garden shifts full circle to him. Qualms of empire
stalled in drawing rooms — worst case, his savagery re-gifted.
Now, as in olden days, Corinthian charity draws God's bathwater
(angels down to the lowliest creature), arguments of enlightened
piety "swallowed up in the infinite immensity of spaces of which I
know nothing and which know nothing of me" — Pascal — and "the
brief span of my life absorbed in the eternity which comes before
and after" — again with the domestic rinse — concluding, "there is
no reason for me to be *here* rather than there, *now* rather than then.
Who put me here? By whose command and act were this place and
time allotted to me?" Because the rapture won't take him — witness
his mouldering smell, gyneform pelvis and trippy dimorphism —
poor excuse for any creator-agency, planned or otherwise.

2. *Res extensa* vs. cookie cutter of hierarchic needs

Or in other words: a less epistemological caveat.
Experiential hope won't make Johnny happy.
Joseph Needham: "An ordered harmony of wills without an ordainer."
Following a chain of appetites from ground-sludge to sunny life force
why not an icteric essence of being that falls between the two?

7.1

There's always someone at a party who, having over-imbibed,
befools a right insult – mon Dieu! Difficult how difficult that must
be away from your frozen waste setting off the dogs next door why
don't they put police tape around you epilepsy straight-backed as
a candy bar raised from the dead no less a shout-out to my mind

Lurch smoothing out his pants   language IS human tissue
too tight down here   bloat thy
                     overfed
outbursts ending in   why
various limbs being torn off said provocateur   not

Stuttering inhuman loves anyone it pays to be wistful when thrown in
the pecking ring – for every EXCESS there's a CHEAP COSTUMEd
emeritus slouch –

He looks up. Evening sets her bottom lip. No one wants to talk.

In his diary he writes:
> *No sex hatched me: to lesser beings was I squired, half*
> *troll, half nun ... a kind of rubber damnation.*

7.2

The hybrid appears

realistic. Intellectual. Social. Conventional. Enterprising. Artistic.

October 1973, Sunset Drive-in: realizes just how studied necessity is.
Naps through *Jeremiah Johnson*, Redford's sleepwalking drawl. Is woken
up by what's initially mistaken for high-pitched jabbering. What he
sees astounds him. Lightning roundhouse kicks, stag leaps and bone-
crunching *coup de grâce*. Bruce Lee's bitten snarl, cartoonish abs.

Cinematic rage writ large outdoors, Lurch is made to feel small.
Having never been prone to his own menace.

Divergent anxiety recontextualizer.

Fugly abandonment breeds outliers. In shamanic terms, an animal-
familiar to remediate pity. One is said to save the tiger or enter the
dragon.

Now do all your jigsaw parts make sense?

Now go through the Body Integrity Identity directory one more time.
Unmothered Type 2.

To what closeted feral class of human do I owe the pleasure?

4.2

Not belonging.

I woke up with assuagement for a birth mother. Her horse rode me
out of nature. She taught me seeds

- eat dirt
- are time capsules
- refute their own air

[mitogen-activated gene altercation?
fluke lightning-strike?]

Summer chokecherries swell the bee's propolis. Sun
to ferment, her sugars bind air, as tracheae in early insects
were said to give rise to wings

where the biggest breath
gained permission   (*noumenon*
at light's soft *habeas*)

the lack of me
(tissue shaped by proxy)
mothered who you are

4.71

Mirrors are monsters I don't recognize — the resemblance comes later.
Did you hear about the guy at the party who —
                              even the talk is forensic.

One learns to put a bag over one's head.

Walk a tightrope.

To enter a body not knowing you enter a unity. The heart ticks towards
god. Where is god's backbone? Pity the raincoats.

Take wisdom over piety, the same thought-induction as electron
potential.

As space contracts around death, the anode is emptied — but return,
a return to what fine splendour — is just talk.

5

Ok let's settle this. We won't speak of it again. So you're in hiding, after another bad-tempered psychological break. Had her lithium receptors been transferable, would bitter doom-and-gloom be a nutrient figment puffing butterflies your way?

1. Chronotope:
   If she seeded herself through you and died, would you say she existed as cause?

The Morpho finds your arm, enters it, and spreads out your palm. Topiary pads tether what's meant. All you can do is excise chrysalis from monster: *We the sexed aerial parts hive what rufous petals might scatter to the wind*

2. Rhetorical continuum [edit]:
   She dies.
   Handholding becomes your music teacher.

   *Estrogen molecules circle their wagons, hydrophobic ends pointed in.
   I should try to think between words. Desolation of mind won't be
   the means by which I end. If my quid pro quo signal-nodes attract
   opposites, what points will ignite? ESTRANGEMENT in nature
   is choice. PASSIVE camouflage versus efflorescence will attract all
   pollinators and reward none.*

5.75

It behooves me to torture what I can't live up to.
If/then statements suck.

As any son's preference inventory might be wont to quell insufficiency
with lament, would a red bathing suit otherwise flatter these Suzie Q
belle-of-the-ball hips, gussied up the withers?

My horse won't settle.
Born hostile to the fray — essentially a secret to myself —

mute solitaire.

5.89

All simile is falsehood.

Oh dancing firstborn, if only I could SPEAK these forms myself, ramified
glia with Jimmy Dean eyes!
The screws in my neck seem not so moundy, they take getting used to, as if
meant to confound epistemes of unsettled difference.

Moon, cascading
that starry ping in my chest
Chinese blossoms click refresh

what an uncritical binary of mind
to realize that I have no breasts.
Ever on to yet another parallel timeline wrapping Buster Keaton swells on
a pentatonic Guttman scale
before hate
                traps evil in its personality.

Tell me I look better in a tailored mommy suit.

6

At first blush, he's cherished the 95 odds and ends of hand-sewn flesh, tints and colours checkering both arms. Not to mention the motley scraps of torso, haunch, nethers, etc.

When they first set eyes on each other, Turing lifted Lurch's veil with these words:

My kind of odds.

Cheap seats to an outdoor boxing match. Someone else's movie. A bookie next to Turing releases homing pigeons like clockwork. With each incoming bird, he deftly removes colour-coded leg bands – fortune cookie–sized bets. These he duly tapes into a pocket ledger.

Statistical unions can't match skill and fitness. But any test pigeon TRAINED TO PECK at the hopper button gets his reward. Three light bulbs on. Not one. Not two.

After losing all bets, they retreat to his flat. Daddy-long-legs trapped in the bowl. Turing wants it flushed. Lurch fishes it out, as if claiming its substance bears the crux.

Stereo-vision postcards. Sepia gloom, lifted.

Mention of an exposed kiss can drag one through the other's dirt.

At their departure, he says to Lurch: *My summer daisy.*

8

May 2014, Glenmore Reservoir, stepping off a dragon boat:
When Lurch is asked, *Where are you from?* his sarcodes aggregate.

A meat-quilt harvest: Filipino, Himalayan, Algerian, Iroquois – he's a
motley clown, a cut-and-paste horror confection sporting a swimmer's
torso. *Little lamb, who made thee?* Cortically mended dopamine to neural
adjunct, vexed catarrhs with all-or-nothing substrates.

Turing, gnosis and probability on his side, only wished him hope.

Egalitarian tribe talk of the longhouse: don't offer bait if it invites
disinterest.
Instead, you deadpan and redirect context.
Flirt the dial tone's inquiry.

Imagines: *One day I'll ride to all those places.*

Waiting for love, his saucy beachside hums for the next – what?
Everything –
evermore.

3

COGNITIVE COG

According to the understanding of identification as an enacted
fantasy or incorporation, however, it is clear that coherence
is desired, wished for, idealized, and that this idealization
is an effect of a corporeal signification. In other words, acts,
gestures, and desire produce the effect of an internal core
or substance, but produce this on the surface of the body,
through the play of signifying absences that suggest, but never
reveal, the organizing principle of identity as a cause.

—JUDITH BUTLER
*Gender Trouble: Feminism and
the Subversion of Identity*

They know not what they do.

—JESUS

UNBOXING THE CLONE

100

I was born not knowing
pitch dark and momentary.
My fluids pooled on Treaty 7
heard the undercry –
      prairie bones
      greater than forced
      burial woke me
      to an *erhu* folk tune on dad's turntable.

I was born not knowing
how church puddings, assisted living
teased from observatory static,
willed one star to circle this wisp of a world:
      extortion lotteries
      on dearly fracked
      buffalo scrub land
      ploughing oil royalties till dark.

Backward falling
future into past, I was born not
knowing why darkness starts under the bed:
      a child opens a book.
      Weaves nuclei
      from absolute snow, populating
      a new page ... and it hatches.

11.1

Embedded in human tissue are trace beings abolished.
Anachronistic codas, from an age of trephined bloodletting.
Lips don't stray
nor do introns' junk-garble sprout foreskins that for trifling sonatas,
get a free pass into our infiltrates' next genome —

waek up Waeymn, wh

ere am I
hven't bin myself in a longtime

indelible wink on numbers and laws, dial tones and shipwrecks, can
spoof a myriad of ex vivo transferases wet-laced by said apoptotic vector.
Already you are the future, born to all futures

from a child's underpulse.
Ditch that and there's war

some poignant detail
raised as its own subject.

What now? Eye-poked and ferreted from a Ming coordinate system,
Flash Gordon's graphite tights would make petri dishes of us all.
Mum to all the archipelagos you can eat. Signature linkages of life mean
to drive patent anastomoses pingponged from Brownian primordiality,
slash-mouths of bored audacity, final-girl enravishments screamed and
queened on brackish shores.
Blame will do, says the snap-on

horror biter's chelicerae
lumbering
against type

11.84

Social environment – what a concept –

Codespread = wordkey.

Base pair deniability flouts the prototype.

Do not share codespread with any other.

You shall have no codespread but your own.

0.0089

eukaryotic mush phagocytized the void
(expansion constant) − (funeral white) = N

Fidelity and truth: open-ended gestures
(my Chineseness) [poignant exhaust touching itself]
amend Rorschachs that stick Cruella on the same easy-listening
chart as Mao, baubles bromating banter from thought-wielding
memes hived in every cell

to beguile fortune
                        you wrestle doubt
(swamp hordes of the Tethys Sea threading telomere to photon receptor)
                                    because

        raising any other
        slug
        is to foil the singularity

2

what would the future see of this polluted
diminution of self, ex machina glitch,
if reason had no clearer sense than to be left alone to ponder,
every Queer Dog Convention richer than castrati

                                                in kinshyp ther
glimflashy lowing subsidizes Snowden's Chinese comedy

                         or is solipsism
                         a subset of unreal
                         McData
                         juxtacrined and morose

                         what would your future see
if you were told you were a black box, and the creator wouldn't
open it because she wanted you to be both alive and dead? Is
resignation enough to satisfy bad potential?

                         I think
                         I'm a condition of the moon, viz,
                         "When we read about a boat we know it
                         has been sunk." —Gertrude Stein

                         Poem,
don't look unless I speak to you. And you in me.

2.3

long ago, human tissue grew Newtonian sails to distance allegory
from its material directrix
                              under guise of woodland
                              breeze on lithesome bowers
            rods and cones plexiformed behind a protein window

tissue breathed, so CO_2 buildup wouldn't bind angiotensins to
stoichiometry, as calcium channels seize,
            some other delicious algebra to expunge those bleak
batons on Pussy Riot

            recursive bruise envy
at the immortal hem of the weaver and the cowherd
separated by their Milky Way
                              only once a year are they joined if
luck in light years [a bridge built by magpies]
            pleases our maker of starry clauses –
                        I mean causes, alignments clustering
            the eye

            pollinating space

2.3002

just to wake up pitiful

                          now

havngnevrbn out of your box

stay please stay   your horse slipping on frost is about as carful

as a fly smaking itself against a window til he breaks

2.804

Sleepy jammies pry open cotyledons at night.
               In a green dream
                  spawned vines lead us to water.

Fifth-century Buddhist texts
set gold and mercury free from base metals
       globbed and inspissated,
                      the plenary mould poured,

            syncytial Rube Goldberg elixir-scares and
psychic boreholes essentialize human to an enslaved
divertissement

from anoxic tissue's liquid/air hooks awaiting further study, minus
the Montreal sinkhole that swallowed an entire family watching
hockey downstairs, minus the view.

2.804 addendum

Look down

                  A child banging pots

desmosomal ions from whatever enantiomeric switched-at-birth
doorstop, helix to cradle, spins eutrophic voids for your sole
honey-eyed other)

                  assayed to bring down the
                  substrate accelerant what

that sloppy yin cooed
new cells   helpless O

                  shoehorned those
                  mesmeric extension thingies

Made in China
feasting on its arrears

7

look up

                    hybrid bloom
        you can't be set apart from what you hate

what of this common strand I speak   down-dragged
effluent   newsy
grace fire
tars lake salt
for the starry grebes of earth, slaughter's downshaft
has nowhere to land but post-European patty cake

arrowhead's feckless
shit-seam turfing its crepes back at you

record that residential school's frozen nativity
sans Orphic
orphan huddled mouthless
while cherubim buffalo
slam their lamps up the sacred

what the sign stirs
from unwritten memory

8

The hatchery's no nunnery. A fated black dot displays the female
virgin. In Fly Breeding 101, liberty will tie orbits to scared exons,
autonomy-envy, plum eyes and curled wings making good by
exceeding their neighbours' bedding standards.

This den of ubiquity speaks to palimpsestuous genes, not always
caring beyond mere tissue how to transact what you feel.

Do you love what you induce? Is event a hormone shuffle from which
blood ties can't escape? If my back settles on land treaties every time
their hammock sways to the soluble antecedent, then who's eating
who, after grid meets underbelly, etherizing science to count twitches
under a dissecting microscope?

He of the poxed complexion mongolizes his phenotype across
banished hordes.

Now leave us our fish and water
oil tankers bungle a savage trade
for this long-winded Indian swindle.

10

You enter a never-ending fight, starring earth's nemesis, Hou-Yi
the purge-happy Prometheus, shooting down nine out of ten
bird-suns. Made emperor, raising a perpetual toast to that
singular kill shot, his MMA windmill punch stops at nothing
to gain immortality. Hucksters and profiteers answer his kingdom-
wide call, while discerning sages flee to the mountains.
Hailed lineage, backdated scrolls on divinity assured, the fraught
vacation continues: Hou-Yi is tricked by his own wife who steals
his immortality pill and sails to the moon.

Through ethers, lenses, gallows' deeds,
extrinsic colossi seem to execute themselves
whether soulful transparency is pure or not, pleasing a world less
sure of its hubris, in search of a following.

Any tyrant must disarm hygiene/pour
on stop codons and bolt cutters/some
righteous analogue music/eyeliner and
enough explosive relief
to corner more pretties —

sure as sunlight fills the world.

3

By the late 20th century ... we are all chimeras, theorized and fabricated hybrids of machine and organism.

—DONNA HARAWAY

Forget that there were monsters. Any master, faced with minutiae, can't sit on his hands. Springtime won't step back. Try hang an angel — body too light to self-garrotte, he won't die. Physical laws, proofs and parables, predicate our fate, reaction-diffusion, incredulous talk. Turing's probability wheel trains the polyglot.

Detach these feet, these hands — rogue instant / linear caveat set to skin base pair encipherment by Lululemon — composite creed from a hair- and eye-colour chart.

Deviance can be smelled, my friends, like boxcar waste chuffed off to camp. If Mod-fab M1 differed from Hellbot A2, you'd be hacking God's source code till the cows came home and still be an unsightly étude for whom it's done to and who gets to do it. Milk Teletoon, fluid dynamics, urban drainage as one-eyed spank hole: a proxy fetish most nightmares have parodied to the point of alien-cannibal and final-girl chase sequences.

You press your remote. I'll press mine.

3.0016

Codespread can't be contained.
From tranquil to domestic gunfire, my metadata rose from her
slum pudding bath, neck-hose and forelimbs flapping.

She came to explain the future.

In the future, all our sun-powered cubicle ceilings glow with
soylent fug that filters our air, dangles asswipe Brillo pads aplenty,
and doubles as mirrors if left to seed.
She lay upon me. Our cables smacked like radio static of a happy
marriage.
Earth, only a fingerbowl away.
Now that rooftop gardens are standing room only, night drizzles.
Quantum froths of cosmetic simportation let us go anywhere –
of course! because you asked –
now who wouldn't tie themselves to that demented frame?

01   00011300 eee 1

Tender plug to my forgotten drain, hers a steady-state scream. Keys and
lynchpins of the academy, words like oeuvre *and* through-pudding
vaulted us into the cortex of yet another fringe organism.
Afterwards we smoked nothing. I fell asleep and dreamt numbers
without sheep. It was all hyperculture, a.k.a. toot suite, a.k.a. soft sell.
It reminded her of retreat. In me it dressed to the left. Soft wired overlay.
Semiotic frags, event-distances.

13

Flouting our world view, earth insists she never gave herself
to anyone.
Our wish, to pull out the shank on another apocalypse year.
Algae-choked
revenue stream
                        manifold miracle
                                    flying a tribe's past arrows
for a future now.
Landfill land, never enough. Slave to institutional gears, why not
scrape your stars into a story robe? Museum screams shrined
in a Metis bell-dress. My friend Sharron Proulx dances without
surrender, sun in tow. But death drags its compass inside her,
this diorama to "tolerance" (aww, cute, sun-braids, too) —
residential buzz cut and roll call —
                                    triage! triage!
Let earth _ _ _ _ _ _ [blindfold].
Riel's heaven opened without a _ _ _ _ _ of ill-gotten [ ].

We no longer name the bringer-of-life. Where surrender named
its executioner, I wasn't told that I was one of them. How do you
(erase erase) do, now let's play together as one family! Talk elides
more talk
                        beadwork
                        in stitches
                        genocide
                        at hand —

Dear future (me included): your metabolic fear — ossicle to
perilymph to endolymph — won't hear her claim.

24

Today's stop and go

             C-train ground to a halt midway downtown.
And the law courts.

Bored by gnosis [logic lies with duty as heretics with ingenues],
everything I thought was "me" vanished when I regarded the mirror
this morning. An overlay of symptoms I no longer recognize.

Psychology's maladaptive phenotypes dream us different. A
reconstituted fetish interiority. What about Lady Justice, reading
with Elizabethan diction? She satins her nose and checks her teeth:
ball-gag of wit, check. Irises

                that lean in like grey monks, check.

Figuring out who you are by what you won't tolerate is like looking
anywhere else but your own mad speech in a vat –
there's so much dumped underfoot, just to keep from sinking, you
learn to step on it. That way, you don't get called on it. Treaties
too. Everything's politely buoyant, winking at the master's light
touch. Often one is typecast to perform the interlude, prepared to
act when acting isn't called for.

14

See how the departed yoke our shroud.

Interim benthic cycles record frabjous humping of honeybees
beneath a manhole cover.

Through whom do the signs bind, and who speaks first?

Take this inadequate arrowhead. It shot itself in the lexicon and
found my hide.

Even a dead word —

Sure as metaphor, right as rain, we will honour our empire's treaty
by acquiescing to a Chinese dinner. Even a dead word looks towards
new life to bear it.

Morning trade in bipolar bitcoin, quarrel and quandary futures ...
such as *meanwhile*. Meanwhile, prayers were heard. Meanwhile, a
blow to the side of the head.

15

All history, mapped in this sonogram: -----v----^-^-v-v^v^v^v^----.

Ducks circle black ponds, hear looped raptor calls, radio attenuation
like typeface talk ... bird
brains also drill for meaning, not fear of it.
What if there'd never been an *if?* asks Dave Eso. Halliburton loopholes.
Precambrian snail, too old to frack a wisecrack for a kingdom, emulsifies
the mantle to her carbon.

Language was our ~~undoing~~ ticket.

What else do you believe? Sea Monkeys? Glinda? Spike belts for milk
runs that fry our hairpins?
Confucius to earth: "keep them in line with the rites and they will,
besides having a sense of shame, reform themselves."

Free will, like free radicals to ozone ...

17

The silent expanses say prayer is but a monk learning his letters.
Dhammapada sees rebirth — not annihilation — as the idleness that
surpasses work.

Science, grim hunchback, leaps from its eleventh hour to rescue pain ...
too late, by some forgone statistic.

If multiplicity rejects narrative, if you fail this holy unction —
if bejesus moment (*couture du jour*),
if Stop, fortune cookie! means you've mastered the noble path —

Ignore these, my lyric outbursts.

The tunnel of love, a darkened Cossack.

18

An eyeball sphere holds no memory, no message.
Only entry and inversion. To see
means frayed substrates eat light. Cymbals
crash, rhodopsins set firing pins to photons,
unblurred from traffic —
young mother on a bus bench.
Child, feet up, hugs her stone girth,
snowed in like a HeLa monolayer. What fun —
my brother shot a magpie. Kicked it long
ago, under
the caragana so we wouldn't miss *Star Wars*.
A child mixes various detergents with dead ants,
dirt flowers, recalls
time capsules banished to the hedge. Moist
fur, then sludge.
Nothing ever seemed to discourage Superman.
Same bus, different year:
a child and mother's
million reasons not to be here,
context beyond light, is
a projection
of failed curiosity.

19

Surging worlds exist for themselves.
They flip up or pause.
Many cancel each other out.

If too much agreement stunts therapy, induce vomiting.
Said the Great Helmsman, *Let a hundred flowers blossom, let a*
hundred schools of thought contend – before rounding them up. That
wilted look of adolescent derailment. Mao-green uniform = hood
ornament, hovering like a mass grave over every rhapsodic hit
parade to repurpose the unwashed. The slim-waisted girls of Chu,
purged by doctrinal good cheer.

In other worlds, you write a poem that's a sleeper cell. It will
drub its tots to find a way out, privileging one chosen
(and one forsaken):
Insta-darling whose sons, bereft of intrigue, model his loud fabrics.

One last clarion: consideration. Not to be plotted, disappeared
and turned over as bedding for someone else's flowers.

20

Tell me?
Ahh, those hooked instruments in my temple.
Flint tools rubbing and sawing. Orange dilemmas of the pre-existence.
This animal spirit locked in an ivory figurine only a moon could imagine.
Waking with hunters' sores, my fig leaf stank of every emission since
childhood. In that dream I ran until I died.

What came before?
In Wonobklekk, our ears are love orifices. From dried *tsuup* stems we
load needle-wasp larvae into the bore, and must chase down, every hot
solstice, mate-companions, the fleeter the better. Deep into the night
you can hear hissing of blowguns and the perforated cry of submission,
as wasp larvae secrete *eklm* in exchange for shelter and earwax.
Without *eklm*, our offspring would be born headless.

What was my line?
If goofy wonders demonize beauty, then there's no more to recommend
the flaw of you being you. And me being me.
Keys to the kingdom? By whose imperial calculus?
Chiral attractants, nimble sensillae, refined company manners.
No wonder we yearn for sky noises to tell us something about ourselves.

Who else knows?
In nature, sound waves attest the owl's dual-funnelled eyes.
Two points of frustration that couldn't see well enough, warp the air that
grooves steady paws, stomping down the warmth.

21

The monster wishes knowledge before boredom,
edom ahead of destruction (bequeathed as an unstated gesture).

Download lacy underage fawning.
Traffic borne of the smallest petal unit, further divided.
The State, invoking the State, tells you
[who you are].

Neighbourhood cameras go hunting Cuban glissandos.
Standard deviation descriptive error:
to wit, your brooding vowels.

Nor do those fleeing reports of, "I escaped pandering" sport economy-
sized yachts. Succinct as breakfasthood, mother's mouth print finds
junior's forehead. Now shoosh. Set his tadpoles to such blistering
heartbeats that, even if they could extol a flamenco of solicitation and
response, the burning wouldn't stop.

The long count
on a short axis.

21.48

I dreamt I couldn't total the winning numbers, because on their own
they dreaded explaining and had to be added up. The official verifier
proclaimed that here, finally, was someone with a method. We trusted
each other through numbers, their discrete valuation crystallized.

Masculine/feminine – what's that? Duped binaries bell-curve
heterodoxy – "tastes like mine" – which never was mine.
O mistress mine, unsex my aforementioned funk. Recycle one
discrete pathology for every carbon unit – no god, no happy death –
only corpse fumes from the vent. Such stars and spangles hover like
mother ships over every Jenner/Kardashian skill set of which I've
never seen the like, lying in their swards.

Not a fad, but the real deal? Do we dare let our humours speak?
Does happy accident breed chimerae, and if they mature into
strongmen, who gets paid off?
Duly noted. With tedious fury, semen approaches ovum like a great
cat, rubbing its frew against an impregnable diastasis.

The age of *Star Trek* and *Charlie's Angels* is Sputnik. Earnest romps
to disambiguate prime-directive shampooing. K-pop spy network.
Warring highlights, set to stun.

22

I looked up. Rain.
A puzzling sight
from before when it weren't nothin'.

Do little
bridge scenes in history
care for such traffic?

Sundry sultry
grope jokes, not mine.
Not your friendly neighbourhood intervention neither.

No
inquiry to jolt new strife.
No sprig

of in
to (expletive) the out.
Like a warm catheter

I let its experiment enter me.

23

This isn't what I chose: bohemian personal ads popping up everywhere.
Chinese responses to politeness. Oprah where she is.
Insistent aged youth, tightened telomeres, groundwater flesh wheel.

What's your birth order. Do McFries eat you.
Please hug a Sherpa.

Until Bruce Lee. Shapeshifter, shit-kicker, rage-sage. A poet lays down
his poem. Enter *light-boned flying Asian pedigree*. Enter *earnest-cheesy
dragon stomp*. Bodies tossed like sacs of Rice-A-Roni, our man will be
an homage to hostage montages spliced with money shots.

26A

Mayakovsky – root or radicand? Hijacked
menu. Into your mimosa print shirt.

Social debt:
1917's minor juggernaut variations let

the dog (spelled backwards) out on a chain.
She wags the end.

26B

Culture factor. Indexed
malware plug.

Inhabit habit where spring's sprung. The ruling class mutates
muteness by what's writ, the rite of it.
Voxel pixels show how punishment, lighting up the nucleus
accumbens, lifts dopamine furor to a revolutionary fervour.

Same difference.
Ask nothing in return.

28

in *Masque of the Red Death*
Poe's strongman turns to his sunny court
of fountain-marooned truffles

rejecting the god of surprise
his sad minions
make merry with the same fruit fermenting the
Buick-sunk marsh whose music died

today we're best served
by pavilion-palavers telling us to keep
the prince cake-fed
safely tucked in his raging galas
knowing pestilence
outside his walls bides its time

and few will dare to leave
their station, or brush by that
tiny breach, for a paparazzi riot

QUARANTINE
for Dave

Gowns or gloves or bleached insistence going door to door
account for streetwalkers
occupying their causes. Snarled
broken hearts versus
canned YouTube laughter, you leave water at her door,
BOGO and YOLO and FOMO lend
irony enough for not just Africa to consider futures –

BOGO because infection tops twenty thousand
you buy one get one as far as bribing delivery boys

YOLO makes a carnival out of men to women to sphinx problems,
light years beneath covers
like a seventh-century miracle drug, *al iksir*, that cures
consumption, the no-more-tears formula

if FOMO's lemon and lifeline twists can't turn plague into an airy,
open kilt
how can fear of missing out make a venous stargazer
out of Joe Fresh, or a stunt pilot out of Ms. Yousafzai,
Saharan teapots at her beck and crawl?

LIFE AND DEATH, BEFORE THEIR TELEVISED DEBATE

zero and Zeno
twin tortoises

slice the instant down to
stillness

from Lao-tzu to Dante's ontic saw

do-gooders say looking up at the stars at
night makes you happy

with life's odious oxides
busy off-gassing
to expansion, I'd rather privatize heaven and pocket
the astonishment

end of life
on training wheels you
should've warned me I wasn't

cut out for this fairy tale
death won't soon
give id
its math key

nor will rise over real
and I've been
good for so long

be a slippery-enough slope
to divide the cousins from their kisses

NO GULAGS HERE

Space Captain Confucius once said, "When those above are
given to the observance of the rites, the common people will
be easy to command," snob that he was.
Smacking gongs and willies with bound feet, one eye to the giant
astral beam that televises hermit regimes,
you'd think he could call down those Disco Starlords any time
over our palaces.
Patting his henchgoat, rectifying piety, what would Confucius
say to Virgos chatting up the ivy, Aries gone emo, milking their
Marley dreads?
The clock ran out on judgment day – oh no, not in the Middle
Kingdom, which gets by on its own – what? Colour wheel?

At Yasukuni Shrine, dark robins kiss the torii thaw as if jumping ship.
Hero spirits widen their Shinto Jetstream, flipping trances with
nest humping
bayonets in Nanking which the push for hydrogen by Toyota
makes Hello Kitty unpin her bobble head for –
why else would Maoists bang pots to scale down birds they'd
otherwise adore in hindsight? A rose smells nice even when
scrunched.
I arrived at death on Friday, permission Saturday, hope Sunday.
Widows afford good intent.
Such inquests for hair-raising obedience can't reform the telling.
But the war-dead might teach us to sing differently.

4

DEVIANCE STANDARD

PANIC ROOM

1

Opposite of panic is happy and polite, so with the same scare that
wracks your fillings, you go ape-shit overwriting someone who
isn't you. He bears your online profile. He ran over someone, not
you, not disliked, not to worry. Who in turn would target you, the
contemplatee, to contemplate the unthinkable

happy is the brain you walk in with, expecting the party will follow
predicted loops

stay low
be mediocre
                    tap emoji widgetry to advertise *On the Make*'s furry
dice in a rear-view, your Axe hair gel failing to register, let alone
poll, voter-qualified opinion

well, no, it's not *that* kind of party
would Steampunk know a cutter from a Nanta's Karaoke hoser, beer-
chugged dopaminergic neurons lighting up midbrain and retina?
Any social straggler would bust a stenography needle
to be in your groove

9

shhh they're listening

press gang full on   consonant-mouth
                    r*t
ekphrastic bod   bed felon
          watch   every
          hypercritical code-suspensor and
psycho footprint
                    y
               vowels vow   tissue   *ohhhh*

                         root   composts   like
               ice needs fission rods
                                        kkk-kk
               claptrap
fetish much?   to police the breach
               when I smell you you
v
     such straight on dignity
                    t*w*t
                    m*th*rf*c**ng poem

          harrowed
          your back

2

Dislike of subject bystander fills the other room not with de-
escalation but with salient profile predictors, i.e., superfluency
versus attitude regression, giggly verbatim tics and bias registers
letting the air out of Billie's blues.
Sit next to me but don't mess with me ... "Sacred fruit sacred
to abstinence" (Milton). Does beauty flirt before dying? – how
disarm eye-batting? Do shoulder pads not divine splendour?
Hangers-on may not want to talk about themselves.

Towards fight or flight, peony muscles spill their sodium out the
PDZ domain, beta blockers ram excitotoxic hissy fits to swell an
aesthetic posse.
Phenomenal differends are synapse mediated on a modulus
consistent with gaze attachment, clocks ringing *I'm late, I'm late*, up
to my ass in beta testing that would flame duck ponds contingent
upon minimal reporting required to administer lead shot in the
breast pocket without the use of a duck decoy.

7

Skull's thick. Through death's plain view of an unbroken occasion, *maybe* hedges the gap.

Red pill: holstered in an armchair. Oh, for a shared strand of evil. Blue pill: paddling Pinehurst Lake to make late beaver tallies in gleaming habitat.

Cornflowers crowd the boat in your head. Think through that hull, to nobbled reeds, loons thrust outside the making of light.

If you were a Chinese U-boat, what would you torpedo for all those TV shows compared to a summer's day? Maybe absence, maybe bulrushes, as summarized by Priestly, via Bentham's "greatest happiness of the greatest number"

[grainy moth-dusk
loons thrusting]

one dormancy bequeathed another
    your *HappyHabbit* app
        dropping you below 0.05
          in Erikson's ego-state development index.

7.1

And the thought of it. The thought of that thought. And –
Too late. Too late.

To remove oneself from sight without being seen?
One featured absence deserves another, brief fire
on the silent black wall behind eternity, everything
                    empty before it starts.

Ice for drinks. Fire starts from nothing. Entropy pulls together
wit from vegetation, occupying equal space at rest.

Who [wysiwyg for street smart] [informal for space cadet]
knew?

No one owns up why.

Too cool for staid, too severe for cool. A speech gun pinches
your nose to wrench open the mouth. Fear stuffs in the barrel like
a Rousseau feline leaping through jugular effulgence, scattering
eternal breath with more succulence by the second

cattails in the dark
shaping loon calls

3

On the Current Events dance floor there's a go-go band with
1/6 s. @ f/5.6 action blur, playing for keeps.

He needs an ANTIDOTE [the category will subsume its gender] to a
panic room, verklempt bosom chesterfield talk about princess jock
nerd thief pathos fuelling our cornflakes at the end of *Breakfast Club*
(the least despicable cool).

"Don't You Forget About Me" sports an Accutane T-zone working to
be popular, not bipolar.

If ginseng tea cured simple minds, if grace iced the room's velvetone
bungee with Hedwig eyeliner, would the de-escalation room seem less
fraught by Heineken-totallers hydrogenating their bunkers against said
under life of the party, he of the C average armpit stain on autopilot,
dumb (*l'attente*) as a lobbed grenade?

3.5

If rage be stalemated or if sweetness haunts the chthonic sea
cave then any task competency belies ample direction drawn
from competing signal contexts in a fluid situation
again the de-escalation room may constitute an untenable
egress strategy exceeding our contemplatee's confidence
index spurned by lipstick hearts void of narrativity
surely he'd rather fixate on the object of his unrest that
according to expansionist temporality befits proxy decoys of the
truly popular whose anxious-ridden status must be cathected
upon such psychic placeholders as said target dislikee

what about performativity
should he breathe with a bag over his head

in lay-down-and-eat experiments the inhibitory effects of a non-
reactive other has shown to de-escalate with some congenial
verve although sequelae have revealed an inconsistency that
few have remarked upon although a reconvened side panel
of pharmacologists have attributed post-anxiety to colonic
distension or too much broccoli or vitamin C megadosing

if that is clinically significant then the internalists have won

4

65% of tested population sample between ages 15 to 25 did
not report exigent escalating attitude in randomized other,
attributable as "enemy" to dislikee, therefore the defining
window of a "crisis situation" did not arise

the significance of a bystander room as a site for collective
decoy intervention could trigger victim multiplicity syndrome
not unlike infrasonic whale music fanning one's redaction to
biodata that solemnly assays, "What're we to do?"
— yet the hostility gradient billows allegorically when starlight
breaks through hushabye clouds and you feel arbitrated by
their Lacanian import, as Morpheus's theremin eyebrows emit
a low buzz riot against those you call hose-hounds — here, we
either clown or gloat

78% of interviewed population felt that gender would play a role
in reconciling target bystander with role of hero/intervener,
irrespective of digestive mood, this being contingent upon
rubbernecking, the HOV lane, and the morning dump

6

excepting our interviewee's strained and tetchy tweets,
footnoting his hyperbaric fugue state over the cheering
commons, we predict x for egg-laying, y for telemarked pity
points, *le mot juste*, Pound's Chinese petals blown free, in
whose segue the muse puzzles

he liked me, see
she says (on all fours, quoting *Grammar Girl*, which can't help
but trigger stereo selective synthases)
but is that really him, or is it truth-acting
you ask (sulk face retaining water)

                    he wants
an ice-ball machine for Christmas, to make softballs and
diamonds clear to their interiority
                    which any party decoy knows will get you
gold-standard wallflower, decidualized and soundproofed in
your post-fetal echo chamber

                    he wants tall drinks clinking all year, else
said contemplatee will affix head-voice whining to the public
apparatus, an exact sitting duck for self-harm as defined in the
DSM that hovers like a mother ship over every minor clusterfuck
if indeed nonverbal cues could splay their marks like ligatures on
a graduated cylinder

he'll succeed if he doesn't make waves

8

Read through dialogic zen with shit-waders
no one knows what
state of ruin can't blame the host

parental misfirings pout like hearts all over his body

the party crowd's jubilant retardation
(Doritos   jalapeno Cheetos   Keanu Reeves)
means that wireless rapture can crowdsource what wit
                you vogue to Madonna-perestroika, cool Warhol
                shades rocking your Che beret

speaking of rock paper scissors
speaking of blue pill red pill
Trojan mammals strut the Xbox floor

the boat in his head glides out to a rose underburn
tinted chinook glint upending cattails
                                how

                                do I conjure who I am

10

Sunset to darkness his tissue screams. Shuts its telescope.

Once he dreamt he was boundless nutrients, connected to the
ocean's pipe. Through him, water cleansed itself and generated
infinite power and everyone bought him.
Before he knew what post-human was, he looked up at the night sky.
Name and operative sign?

                    Bruce Lee.

                              Hospitable bruiser.

Soon, busyness freed his sense of cliché. Insufficiency drew him to shiny
things — as if supreme inadequacy with the sequinned sky's analgesic
stop-clowns stunned every waking nerve of this billion-webbed hiccup —

*everyone bought me and checked me out — the yin-yang, the subject-object — don't
they know Cthulhu read Siddhartha? What hero is virtue without fear? If I can't
be you, two-by-two, then who approves the bait-and-switch?*

Now, all grown up, freshet phthalates and Azocyclo-V8 bitumelons pour
through him like soft basal blather relieves human tissue of its silhouette.
And if foreseeable devastation quacks like a duck, then why *shouldn't*
everyone be sucked into his eye of catastrophe?

8.4

When we're alone the amygdala striatum craves dopamines —

tigers of restraint pound sweat into my pillow and don't we all feel like
students these days what with pupating pneuma, neon efflux, gang pangs?

Ergo sum of all excitable genes my titillation's a placeholder for, why
isolate the object (me) from brain-eating salivas that can't unglue their
polemics, let alone cry me an impasse other than this product-placed spam?

My orifices tell me, sir,
you aren't the only one.

8.88

In view of a salvific norm, the hall mirror you ignore next to
a Grecian urn can't upstage what ready-made mist from the
catwalk sithes

the de-escalation room's serendipitous slipstream sets everyone
to eat each other unto consanguinity
until a savage commons stands alone

delinquent neutrality fleshes ego to soul to quintessence to spirit
and by retrieving yourself through such filters
aren't you still cherry-picking what you really really want

Cheshire   spyware   scareware

when locomotor memes rejoice like cramps in Shanghai, dogs
and pilgrims press their ears to the jazz

8.5

A bat scarfs my ear. Sonar sweeps part your hair. Whosoever grows
teeth will do what sex wants.
Rise from your pained dish. Soup flies don't tunnel love like those
nihilistic flobs do at the Stardust Market.

A tongue dives under ferment to predicate prevaricate I mean countervail
its sound print, chaste unbuggery charmed by a chorus of avenging
trumps. Since when did your scruffy endorphins ransack modesty?

I'll wager if one stays the course by blending schnapps with selfie updos,
more Ziggy wayfarers will swoon to fury like hypertriggers.

That pancosmic seam in my underwear tells the girls I'm cool.

9.12

The room not capsized he enters. Hotbed of self-censure,
clairvoyant dread: will fidgetry play louder than overture,
part decoy, part mercenary swagger?

Score. Shore.
A retreating pie. Say goodbye, fireweed, time to woolgather.
Sky nearly autumn.
Elk scat anchors clover at the foot of a lady's slipper.

In that room, blue funk does Dallas to a Bach Variation —
some jackboot bilge-wetter, some stabby little number by
Xena the sword plunderer.

9B

a panic room's goth darklings flip Tourette's with spoonduggery
while trading barbs of eroding status /
initially the bait room caper, tasked with wan-faced cheer
dragged from boys dissing Mozart, has bloomed into an overt
exhibit of canonical import /
polity-grade factory jocks lay down their mothers' Buddhist
freeloader grins, a pointy heel protection program occasioned
by residual eternalism through the 60-inch TV sphincter

psycho-normative poser
clown dish

said the bodybuilder to the mirror
I'm so lonely I can only get bigger

you fall serum first, wastoid by race titration, how urbanely
one's Colour Correction Kit Canoodler stumps giddy-yap with
wetted daze and a sunflower for the host, whose locker room
hazing might not win more friends but at least get you invited
to future shindigs

10.4

it seemed trivial that a no man's land could be attained by simple
arrival, straining one's canoe over virgin estuaries, parking it and
laying new eyes on an old normative halo, yes to earth's booty,
sippy straw out further than any recorded continent

chai latte's franchise plants my seed-metropolis on a first-glance
shore, breath sure as some eagle cry that we're never simply
ourselves, draft dodgers tired of empire, tranquil and blameless
we took everything for granted at first contact

so easy to say We're Home, Honey, boneyard unswept, how
musical railways end pacifism, prime location subject versus
windmill or any such unprovoked exclusion howl standing
our high ground, plague-robes bartered to end grief

STORIES TO START A BAD TRIP

milk and meat go bad in warm weather so might I suggest you
UPLOAD the deed   check slyboot wannabe at the door
Boy Scouts act out   scenes of hunter-gatherer revenge pardon
that goat for having breasts we carry our grandmothers
the Khanty of Siberia have shamans speak to animal totems and
hitch rides as reindeer spirits guiding those lost to the gods
in their frozen sky

FREE MARKET TAKES BRIBES TO BEG OFF TROUBLE

don't plug my mu or kappa receptors with Velcro if dongles strap
dynamite there's no opiate quite like home is what the neighbours
say   cupid clamps hickey ~~on anxiety~~ on dyskinesia not some
hysterical dishrag stuffed in the mouth for ransom

MORE BLACK HOLES THAN EVER

one learns to build permission on the futility of others seizing the
daily coup   axe swings propel the next incarnation's analgesic
tuffet rhyme and little boys blue   one bad eggy starts the
baby rolling

4.04

In our future together you unbutton my shirt and I levitate.
Does the noise in my head bother you?

In the room, the contemplatee's pillow-to-knife reunion
spurns his love's adjunct to care, only to be repelled and cut to
bits as a form of inquiry.

What of the banned substances in divers' spermaceti?

(There will be occasion, lighthearted estrangements, like kicking
a shot magpie under a bush, but he won't find it in the trenches.
Do floor stains count? Is bursting wastedness? Can bystander-
decoy rage be an off-leash rejoinder with nothing to lose?)

101

This room   exile   exit   in this
one calm doorway   before   after

you say okay but your astrocytes say
that's not it   that's not it at all

Nietzsche says we need to be more like cows
"and learn the art of slow rumination"

if I can be any   body   I'd be some
one other   (than)   what I refuse to suffer

POST-MORTEM

Were you technically responsible for any of it?

Were you of sound [   ], temporarily [   ], where litmus blue
saw red, foment to de-escalation, and back again?

At one's bedside are alternative glosses of reports of accounts.
Years pass. A leaf shoulder. A pool gloom. Panoptic levity, therapeutic
lensing, will bend our taut logic over fever charts. On a good day,
Tony-the-Tiger endorphins absolve human tissue of its catalytic.
Bad days, the world's cold fusion will be powered by guilt alone.

Where *Das Kapital* takes weed seriously, no
declaration of freedoms includes a contract on safety.

Did someone say, *martial arts substitute?*
Insomuch as it was of no use to anyone.
What is owed to society in relation to the body's
defence, vis-à-vis intentionality?

My thumb, said the president, had nothing to do with that trigger.

5

MUTE
FUNCTION

Only a total stranger could ask such a question. Are there control agencies? There are only control agencies. Of course they aren't meant to find errors, in the vulgar sense of that term, since no errors occur, and even if an error does occur, as in your case, who can finally say that it is an error.

—FRANZ KAFKA
The Castle

It is only for the sake of those without hope that hope is given to us.

—WALTER BENJAMIN
in *One-Dimensional Man*
by Herbert Marcuse

LAST ONE STANDING

When Dad passes on
who will be left to argue
about consent?

I'd forgotten when I reached for his remaining foot
after cutting his first five toenails
that he'd lost that foot to ischemia.

Rain pools on cars at Tim Hortons.
A large earthworm noses its way across,
won't be long before it meets a tire.

No orderly to help him pivot
off the toilet, he leans to one side, pulls
his pants on, scrubs his teeth.

You need two to disagree and two
to find your way, I mean keeping
things real, that phantom feeling alive.

When he's gone I'll be fine.
I'll cross the same parking lot,
notice a lone chopstick in the gutter

its function impaired. Of course
they'd throw it out. One
attains parity. Last

one gets even.

THE WIDE-RANGING SPACE HE ALWAYS WANTED

a time-scaled glaciation

river-blue skies   along the   parched

castanozem   haze-bound dunes ride semi-arid steppe

sweating in kitchen heat   my brother the polymath   reads
stirring tomato beef   Dad flips eggroll skins

alluvial fans and fanglomerate   ghosts play door buzzer to
slick shouting feet entering or leaving   Tasty Chop Suey   low
light outward Peggy's Cove Fish and Chips and Prymak Optical
Richmond Road's fortunes flow by

                                cash register lights-out
glimmer to soda fountain whose starry outline scars the traffic
between us and Motorbike City

when he's not soaking toilets in ammonia or pushing a broom
my brother hangs out with Dan at the motorbike shop   otherwise
he sips a milkshake and reads about Ferdinand von Richtofen the
Red Baron's uncle   who surveyed Tibetan ranges exceeding
the last magma outlines of the Great Wall

south of the Russian Altai there's a paradise river whose fluvial
sediments can be traced by prevailing chin towards the snows
of Qilian Peak   from there to Silk Road   caravan Genghis to
Attila's plateau cliff   meander   the years' entanglements

look up   the land wants to call itself Gobi but not where the
old frontier   Gaxun and Sogun Nuur Lakes   meet stream
and sagebrush that echo deer

            he drops the broom and the book   come here
pushed

through swing doors   slapped   not tomato-prawns   not
number 89   number 85 tomato-beef   enough wasted
money here to wash the floor with

what did Dad want? (tiptoe repair, not this push away from,
this defection)

tames earth to vegetation   one plight in-
distinguishable from an other

                            my brother's not reading he's fuguing

and to be quite honest   when he's not here is like
craving plum sauce without the eggroll

I too, begin to follow that river by horse

Dad snatches my brother's library book from my hands   throws
it into the garbage   pours deep-fryer fat onto it

a month later without fuss my brother will pay the Calgary Public
Library $5.95 in damages

                    the restaurant of our childhood
          Tasty Chop Suey   no longer exists

for years he kept that book at the bottom of his drawer

rancid pages   ink bled through both sides

I'm sure that the Gobi ranges of Turgen-Kharkhiraa in the summer
of our longest day   murmurs with tiger weasels

if away is just a chemical mirage

                         not

                         us

BUT I'M NO ONE
for M. Maylor

Dear Anne Carson:
My friend read me the poem where your mom
said that the dead walk backwards.
You thought this myth arose from poor translation.
I can attest to your misapprehension.
My social studies teacher in grade 8, Ms. Rogers,
believed it was customary for the Chinese
to walk backwards when entering a washroom.
So when our class went to Silver Dragon for lunch,
that's what we did, giggling, even if we didn't have to go.
But in my family, we never believed this.
Where do ideas like that come from?
It's true that regret looks back, that death's shadow follows
us, and your only true companion is solitude,
whose clarity will fade to black.
It makes sense that the face of death must
be turned our way. We're still here.
I have to read lots in order to find
what's useful, Ms. Carson.
To walk backwards is to safeguard not knowing: in the end,
my striving can't reach more than this. Than this.

BINARY OCCUPIER OF THE 1%

                            0000.00   – hey you

class   trap

lone words   heartfelt   for

        claptrap   tent city

  versus some rubber-stamped Runnymede parchment

           window grazing   queer adjacency

                     alley-oop

000

           ether gears sproing   from

           nervous trail mix can't help but

                              be   my

diminished   recursive   pleez   *nourriture dans la terre*

             survivalist rage   some recycled

stoner wearing

  whatever I say. When I · say   it's Hey You.

If not for placards and bottles everywhere

        they'd blacken my copy

              candles 000101 out

Calling All Occupiers

     fall on your empties   peaceably cuffed or removed

               bullshitty

               whale slinky

officer   mob   eco
        sophist   Hobbist   ergo
            fries and diet Coke
arbit   orbit   Arbus

                neocon flash card

    nimbyist   peace   that
    surpasseth dead occ
    espies astigmatic

            carnival stigmata
                            hey you

01   iii   01001
0011

heart on   heart off

Arkham loving

class

brawl   pamphlets form fit

domo reparando at City Hall   stereo

Rita Hayworth's bomb in loyal congress to stardust   for
the   good of   for
Good   this country 'tis
perhaps effigaic of some henchbot's folderol on shale oil
barometric fields of disbelief borne out by aerial mapping

$<@"#

was all

I ever

owned

a.k.a. Milgram's flux dial on cousin May, she'd never hurt a
fly

apartheid berries from Olympic Plaza
sprout   slave bandwidth
tell me what
subprime will succeed our Party Whip, hoicked between
blanket fort and mission control

0030002

however briefed   you lay   last summer's
                           afflicted grass
will dig through choral thuggery owed

       brinksmanship   our   new Eden
                                   snaked
          by shaft-hardened yes troops

     tips for aiming SETI mirrors and self-pleasuring antennae
          on the centre that can't hold
          space in my head
                   the o in zero and god

    Delibes's "Flower Duet" left private smell markers,
no gc.ca mole wassailing our e-trail

    entire continents off the grid

world-building is to freedom what Stockholm Syndrome is to
rowing another refugee ashore —

same scare-to-signal ratio of some sleepwalker
bearing the turbulence of his own demeanour

what would it have taken
                    to re-enact the valour if one of us were a wet noodle
                            camera shy
                                    truncheon

                    (who

owns whose ass) beaten with chlorophyll sarcomeres
        framing
                    public   edict
                            an ego
                                            in-service

www.http://0.004400000171

Dear Corporation:

Compared to blind, dumb, and dirty, the aerial part of a flower is
what breathes above ground.
Its heartbeat in your face.
The aerial part listens for sun energy.

The aerial part entreats gods, not bandwidth PR. Not effluent
sired by some soul-sucking blue suit.
Their breath, become destroyer of worlds.
Words have feely tails. Surveyor contracts core them with paper
rights to land. Any further fuss will shear off facial tics at the root.

Failed tub liner, reeds
in leaked tailings: move along. You do not [   ] here.

Say yes to frack water. It flings its meniscus at tar birds and
water-bears, how
did seismic lines buffalo-jump place for people, tipped off
Crown Land – chickaboo thaumaturgy, so crude it seemed
lazy? Now owned by a dark syndicate.

Forget the pre-existence. Tomorrow's baseline price for bread?
The 1% mop the poor with it.

Same swooning patriots who tip too much and brood too little.
Let bygones, your freedom-through-work, lead us.

With better brains, we can decide not to host what ails us.

IMMIGRANT FREEZE

frontier faiths are jealous
just a glimpse of the new world
makes my grief mere hopscotch

what tomorrow sells
sticks an app on it
I pull out my exhausted legs

every drowned noose and
tribal abusement pumps
stale container breath

I've a ghost conscience
urine-scorched walls like
blotting paper carve a scar

initials remain
with or without invoice
our cries go cold by morning

TONIGHT, LUTHER KING ON VOCALS, MANDELA ON SAX

So raise your voice. Hang extra ears to hear.
Blackbird insists, honey-eyed
getaway from strange
loud fruit. How now,
ally rapster, rallying leaderless ragtime
to better my solo?

I'm not dead. The gun
to my head scats
prison notes, rival echoes. Night
muse? There you are, pouring yourself
in chains
as they bell out that hep-hop swing.

Jazz craved what ghettos ached,
confounding scripture.
Is that freedom? Can
lawn crosses in homespun syncopation
stomp for all of Africa?
Go ahead, try me

from goldmine to
cotton gulag for tired harps, let
morning say amen to our half
note, down
for breath lest
we forget: *sweet dark. Run boy. Run.*

SIX MEMOS FOR ENDURING TORTURE

1. FORGET

After the first jolt   what a banal cry

                          heart   to head one line
     yours, mine   after
          hair and skin flay the interrogator
          embarrassing us both. If we are   joined
                                   I promise
               rest will come.

This line, head to heart, is a lie. To yourself you don't belong.
If you're wronged, there's no one here to commit. Due process,
that old term, cauterized and corrected – you chose that. Only
the neck feeds head to heart. Its psychic reconstruction a pink
stump. Your neck gave me permission to use it.

If I reside as your object of disappointment, then I'll have lost
the occupational advantage of representing your necessity –
only then, rest comes. Our words say nothing –
leprechaun. Spectacles. Chlamydia. Beach ball.

What they used to mean.

2. DOCUMENT

X out. In out
white noise. Allowed. To sit. Standing not   talking

        while kneeling on. Glass. You are a regular person
        kneeling on
                innocence begs exile or guilt
                            A
                regular person's confession includes

                (I
                understand)   *beyond*
                        good and evil numb the gap

        Or else:
confiscate thumbs. Hygiene. Lord may

fray   everyday   electrodes. Plug in the poem. Spell it:
truth!   t-u-r-t
        sorry. It really hurts me more than

                        plead uncle plead regular person plead

3. BARGAIN

Roll with the punches, Lone Star. Don't say "ouch" as if it were a
blasting cap for anything. Just yesterday you were all smirky and
hooksome. Wrong pogey bait, sir! One chooses the scene for which
begging electrifies

     (you know

          you will)

so step outside. Stir a Persian garden with gooey snails, fattened on
milk. Milk of amnesia. These snails root me to the ground – propped
up, pants open. Are the snails intestines that don't know me?

What metaphysical surgery have I survived?

Pubic rain clench. Make it go away.
Am I a south-pointing meat-arrow everything leverages to tarry a
shuddering collapse?

The tip of your meme won't last.
Go with the least harmful version.

4. REFLECT

Evening river.
Small shrivelled placentas for every rosehip
clutching last year's stem.
Funerary tunnels'
don't know what to do with themselves.

How do you speed away from it
you season-swept fairies of necessity?
Bees to their hollyhocks? Not yet.
Always outside a garden
I'm hallucinating.

Twist the peony's neck for
clarity of introspection. Does *to be*
not know what plus what equals heresy?
Another three twists.
Which of the nine levels of your exam

shouldn't be put to the question?
You know what we're looking for here.
Unburden. Fess up.
Bend toward what you know in your heart
bears forgiving.

5. SLEEP, or, WHEN GOON SETTINGS LEAVE YOU IN A TIZZY

Fade to movie black
insomnia sea to river
beats you like a slug

sheep lose count
legible furs and
Nu Shu and stars

if you start crawling
think say hovel under
remind me what I want

if social parlance
were to critique itself
rubber hose to mouth

6. IMPERSONATE

Say you did it to yourself is disagreeable. Say you did it to others?
An outright lie. Say you did it to the future is partly true.
Let me count flesh's parting: transected by our apparatus, it squirmed.
It registered. Logy nerves startled till a garden bloomed for all eternity.

Tease open that shirt or skirt. If benevolence chooses style over cut,
what passes for blood? Ketchup? A finger's delectable crawl through
tight eyelets? Imagine. The sorry world without its frivolity, if not for your
antecedents, lobules, and simmering underthings – neatly tucked away.

Any artful line I draw will determine whether you reside as a person or
its object. I've even put a box in your head so you can fill it with god.

Lights off now.
Time to face your edit.

At the end of the tunnel, you'll see.

6

BEHAVIOUR
RECORDING

EVOLUTION OF KAFKA'S HARROW

Pulled hard the river's edge, one night remaining. Wildlife's
hiding place.
Boreal catchment claws out the ridge. Winter's back
molars
      flossed wolf trail
(fallen ventriloquist snow)   patience
                                    not
                                    bareness
circles to find glacial drainage.
Between Sisters' peaks, words pike like stars,
so few tracks. Grouse down. Blue
robes exiting the world's ledger.

      For instance, kente cloth,
seasonal plant dyes, talismanic lozenges
hew rivers out of bird's eye views.
Tactile zoetrope
spun from
spit and genes.

It was a story to rid me of pain.
Tubman's hymn in a small boat certainly opened the referent gap.
Poplar Neck to Wilmington to Philadelphia.
Escaped rhetoric to anneal the past.

So the story goes, self was fast fading and had to find other,
had to make sense of this floating centre from which
stars and weathers circled.
Propitiation at the garden shutout,

the loud stellar bookkeeper catalogues
falling spirit-capital to feed our moral solitaire. Negation
being the perfect loves-me, loves-me-not
dope fiend to replenish soil.
I still don't think I'd want me
if I met myself at the footbridge of light —

an early finger-poke broke a drop of mercury into identical-sized
satellites.
One of us dared to feel with our tongue when Ms. Grodeland
wasn't looking, its acid shock
parameciating three dimensions from two,
grade 5 chemistry hoarding a pile of broken thermometers
drained of curiosity,
like adult bird spew building a nest, that what my friend Harvey
in his Buster Browns said was true —
what the man upstairs told him: no Holocaust
the boat stopped at many ports   no one wanted them
and I tried to figure how to make
good from bad, should our friendship end, when the man
upstairs told him
that our books were wrong.

Space-time paper, warp and weft of rug-telling.
War needs repeating, freedom through labour to
build team spirit on this day of vacuum-sealed meat violations —
with full nests
hatching one doctrine
there can be no emptying.
Poetry calls on other worlds to interleaf this one,
two ventricles from one. Exhale
the perfect day —

what's that you smell? Cottonwood
fluff, daytime wraiths blown over a residential
school field with nothing to follow, no one to come and play —

hhhhello   or
               hhhhelp

nature trails gone cold, honed and scrimmed
faces slide back into chemistry without fuss or unction.

Lanterns burn above the Ganges
where human waste balances her pH
until your mother ship takes you back
to live among the pure.
                      A declaration of intent:
fascist futures differ only in applying the golden divide.
When rule becomes ruler,
bottom line hits scree. Weight of rags,
don't
let this soft universe go through you first.
Any griot knows not to repeat the old saw,

Eve lifting her eyes not knowing at first what creature from that
water returned her gaze.

Harriet's escape route mentions wetland dragonflies. Row the
Choptank River to Chesapeake. Safe house in Ithaca. Rochester.
Onwards to Niagara Falls, beneath the lion's paw.

If it were up to the animals, paradise would be just too new an
idea to be talked about in a useful way.
Even birds will wing it. Do they ask, where?

That's why ultraviolet landing strips, on their way from kings and honey
gatherers, entreat us.
Many points between, gutter to kingdom come, seem glad but withdrawn.
You learn to follow water, what with the extinction jokes. Not to mention
the accused.

       Inside our empire, green resistance grows —
birth, sleep, retreat. Dialectical animals
teach all and leave none out,
     solicitude and stratigraphy
     servicing a free ride.
Maybe silence can now defend itself against those who stayed quiet,
and those who died —
phonemes, horses,
conflict residues and failed shebangs —

Harvey got into Automotives in high school, new friends,
girlfriend, and as far as I could tell, kept those views to himself.
I found out later that there really was a man upstairs, a teacher
who boarded with his family.

It waits for a propulsive link or a Wet Paint sign:
VIAGRA. MICROBEADS.
No consensus downstream, cows neither here nor
chewing against the rind. Tree sap,
lifeblood to queens' cup —

shhhh. Hushhhh
                   (we know
it frets at vectors, uptakes, enantiomers,
tasked by tastevintners and inquisitors,

pida, vedana, ruja,
to squeeze, to know, to break open)

even in Sanskrit the weapon used against you
is muscle-nerve fatigue,
nociception's gold filling teased from the grin on the rack,
tissue harrowed to text,
inscribed penance for cab fare

else who
will pass muster before the lord of alternate endings?

Will inversion shock buskers who know you better than you
know yourself,
percolated by Monsanto, dry rant, et cetera,
agreeing that the Shenzhen pillow-stuffer stuffs for the
common good,
no new sunset to ride into?

A story robe or shroud can map a body, an arrow,
striations beating slime
to the poem's end trajectory.
But the poem reads itself,
razed and raised
in and out of mind again, as if to say,

Now, Truth. Now, Meaning. You must go.
        Poem = bare nest. Who
remembers you anyway, when shorebirds black out, done flapping
and darkness swallows the word before its song?

Let what pampered us
nix gopher talk for what delicate threads we are,
spun from land and blood,
finished by their telling —

under this enormous bowl of sense   what then
                                       will your home
              your home and memory   be?

TO BE, THEN NOT TO BE

 Leamington's defunct Heinz Ketchup factory,
its brick-font smokestack
fixed without seeing
a black widow's red hourglass to rival warning.   The male
 plucks her web to talk things over.

Venality of milk, tea, coffee
everyone has a stinger   (when I was small I could fit into the
Hoover vacuum box
 later I would traffic in excuses
for a Cat Stevens CD).

 In my palace
of deranged reunions, the throne of my grandmother
is kicked over. I saw her only three times – once, in bitterness.
She hated Dad, believing him   (after drinking? gambling?)
 to have caused Mom's cancer. The only time
 Stepmom brought me to visit Grandma
I was warned, don't talk about your sister, the sister
 who married a Dutch idiot.

Grandma hugged me. The rest of her family
 (my uncles and cousins) had gone swimming.
They weren't around to receive us.
Stepmom gave me an ultimatum – you leave with me now, she said
 or stay, and find your own way back to Calgary.
 Grandma promised that I'd be okay.
Guilt-ridden, I cried.
 We both cried. Soon, the uncles and cousins

arrived and we played soccer, ate corn, quail eggs, and shrimp
all their names forgotten.

When I got my licence a decade later I drove to B.C. and saw
Grandma but she wouldn't stop badmouthing Dad, Dad's
brother in Maple Ridge wouldn't stop either so I told them off
exchanged
safety corridors for a passport, alone
with that invincible high road

do I teach my own kids this when they see Grandma
for their first and only time?

Let's not talk about the whys
aged 96 she enters the spacious den of her new Vancouver
Special, opens her arms wide and proclaims, where are my
great-grandchildren?

She always was a great kisser.
Love for her
was severe, a tooth my tongue kept catching.
Naah, m-gek-thlai nee-ga meng,
she'd laugh. *Ahh, I can't remember all your names*

for all the years of toil and discovery

EPISTEMOLOGY

When someone looks at you, the mind courts stillness. A string
of finials. Chu Yin studied by the light of a bag of glow-worms,
selling bee organs, hyacinth blues, one more carnival haunt.
Dad, I see your capable variations on a summer day:
lake-hauling + sweet spot = carp caught in a bamboo pipe,
thumping tails poured out this morning. An eye for a telescope.

Clearly, the undersea dragon king is wooed, though my uncle's
adjective-heavy story would scatter ghosts of future Cains.
My niece tells me: machete in hand, you chase your brother
down rice fields, banana and mango (murderous), past
flooded marsh to Hoi Seng's bush-meat market where a sagely
cowled pangolin beseeches you (half-crazed) with a Mae West

purr — *so who's the dark prince here, boys?* — meaning, there are
fixes for unaired family grievances. Were you trying to teach or
kill him? Doesn't look good for my kids either waiting for an
answer, my uncle nearly in tears and his daughter and her oily
husband smelling blood, asking your son at their fine reunion
supper table. But all I can say is: *Your guess is as good as mine.*

NIGHT-BLOOMING CEREUS

What is it enters, finds us
those stars that we might pull from it
distant life? So that nothing
shared comes closer than this heart, sure
beyond hope that we'll continue Out There?

      Motif. Moonflower one year. Then
      mimosa, wilted to the touch. Resin-
      lidded cells twist the jar on a life
      stilled, as I move the electron beam

across a fluorescent screen. One draws
from conglomerate memory
whatever moves us to stop
hurting. So we divide and don't stop.
Goniometers hum. A flower

      won't say how its reckless bulb
      grouts out from a serrated leaf. Spearlets
      globe to a white bouquet, petals
      nearly drooping the minute they air out.

Carousel. Tropism. Things
you can't catch: reason, necessity, the
causes — did you really think you had a choice?
What I can't help
becomes no choice.

ZERO

Reading this I read my own mind.
Slow crowding lichens doomed the process
of asexual reproduction I guess.

Like a siren, or some small spider jumping
my eyelid to yours, we've
matched the groove of the placeholder —

the zero so few knew what to do with,
led us into this space
neither fills to exceed our grace.

Disable a sibyl. Dispatch Wang Wei. At
presto, 1 divided by 0 makes gods of light
vomit dark matter. Infinite

stepladder amazes the same
worry spot where floors disappear and
stars frolic in folds of time

faculty and nonsense
streaming forever. And so
we dream to exist, before we do.

7

TACTILE GNOSIS

ENTER THE DRAGON

1

11 p.m.   looked at myself as if
I were a complete stranger's
shadow   clinically disengaged
they throw my Kato kicks back at me

so I move on   execs tap Carradine
must lean on forms and means
deduce the shortest attack between two points
deception focuses scrutiny

to my heart's untied ribbon
given cha-cha lessons   we become one
gaze unbroken when bent   if
a bird lands does my astrology weep

for that untrained body more beautiful
to the world than hopeless sorcery
minimal lines of energy can be taught
killing can't

2

The touch of death informs
my one-inch punch
(except for Norris) Saxon and McQueen would
think kicking's too girly
trapped motion the failed longhand
we who would cast off circumstance

on practice mannequin or blood jukebox
poured to shape   I'm losing weight
will everyone turn to judo instead
and rest their brotherhood
on an aptly schooled
uniform   you aren't

where your present body goes
let the elbow block and hit in one stroke
still here   we haven't
yet grown the soft butthole between
our eyes   once that happens
I'd venture to say we stay awake forever

3

Ha! He has big muscles but they're not efficient
to be oneself and unchanging is stillness
to have nothing in you that resists is emptiness
detachment from outside things is fineness
and no contraries inside you – purity

punch = distance ÷ rhythm
the classic ghost rupture
on film where you live and die young
even birds to their birdbaths
under cover of retirement

don't mind those coddled on hate
everyone's a stagehand to their own
B-movie *arrrgh!* with flailed *hai-yahhhh* –
just think of me typing summer screenplays
the warm breeze pleasing itself

for old times' sake you cheer when fists of fury
unmonk my beast from handcuffs
note the more flowery *gung fu* that looks
better for TV   just one
more face the medium can't kill

A PARABLE

The hunting spider played dead when I smacked it with a book
by Graham Greene.
Half an hour later it righted itself, checked its hinges and
started crossing my bedroom carpet again.
It had won. Too scared to touch it, I blew it under
the fridge.
One sacred text mentions a bent arm for a pillow.
Trouble and deprivation can be soft-hearted.
That night in my pyjama party dream, Mom
was nowhere to be found.
Everyone had gathered round the large aquarium
to see a brown clam hanging off a wedge of rot.
I said, *Who wants to see a new life form?*
Sugary strings vibrated those singing clam-lips.
The creature next to it was even more enchanting,
a Venus flytrap elegantly sprawled.
Piled at the ridge of her florid mast were two scarlet rows of eyes
that flashed hard at us. She wore a crown of blue stinging
bees that buzzed at our faces, daring us to defend
our curiosities where they weren't wanted, but
try as I might, I didn't detect indignation
from either creature on display.
Which meant that the burden
to soothe and not wear out the only
welcome they were ever going to get,
blank parsecs across oases of intelligence,
fell to me.

FOR YOUR SHOPPING CONVENIENCE

Those were my salad days, taking down a roomful of thugs. Do
you see how all forms, poured from struggle, dance? Art is never
decoration or embellishment. It is a constant sense of maturING
(in the sense of NOT [having] arrived!).
Losing sleep at Roman's. He's always after some girl. Getting
better on skis, but not with the group ... now for once I'm
looking at the jet set from the inside out.

The Pakchong director's unbearable air of superiority. No
meat ANYWHERE. At least I have vitamins. Boxing teaches
adaptability and rhythm of attack.
After *Longstreet*, Paramount's offering a thousand per episode.
I'll want to double that.
I was born into the theatre, where pretend and The Way
interchange. Every night of *Golden Gate Girl*, Dad brought me
out on stage in a dress. Soon I'll be leaving for Singapore, to ask
forgiveness from the elders. Making reservations now. HK films
need more quality. At last, you can depend on me.
Ted, listen. The name, "Enter the Dragon" suggests emergence
(entrance), of someone (a personality) that is of quality.

[   ] such that perfection can be a sore loser to success —
Give "Me-me boy" a kiss for me, and baby Shannon too.

With love,
China James Bond

LEGERDEMAIN ON CITIZENSHIP

Towel on the face, towel on the head:

after Harper, there's still an Arctic Circle
                    so why shouldn't foreign (and this ain't
            your mom's bandana for sure) coverings
                pay a thousand and one slights?
        Treaties are old hubcaps. Avast,
                    ye mates, This Land Is Our Land
                        one
                            less
                            talking circle

fair Democritus scattered by poker-up-the-knickers
niqabbery to

                        conscript
        order interruptus   (read terror)

what Eve lost was a self-winding tomahawk (of the
Old Stock Canadian kind) – when seeing her reflection
and pulled towards self-desire, Adam's ministerial
voice warns her that her love must be his, for thou
"shalt bear multitudes like thyself" – amen. As merry
men follow, Stats Can and Fisheries libraries proved
"access deni'd" shorthand for prorogue deniability can
can any reasonable doubt on State Certainty

        any rhetorically harrumphed
                        lord politico

riding his riding
will circle-talk nice hair
and find no news here.

As for our sadly deported, *Where's Waldo* will keep 'em
guessing on this post-Milton Monday:

"Hee for God only, shee for God in him" – to face the
true face of our great land, ye vassals –

       once fair Democritus

       wringing his spheres

?

Ask a hungry puddle   how old is
                                                freedom
if dying

                                can transmute
                        sorrow   if in fact
this finger is the one life you get

                        wrinkled starlight
                jumps in asking
        to distinguish source from arrow

                                window frost
        aims to
        reflect
                If only one
                                could see
                        past

                        this
                        .

ACROSS THE FIRMAMENT

Ride the final journey by horse.
When Enkidu is permitted to meet Gilgamesh
he climbs halfway up, reaching his twin, who,
in tears, descended halfway –
one touches flesh. The other, bone.
The bottom drawer of Persian rain
softly coupled.

Knocking off dead
blooms early
a warbler shakes off her snow moustache
whistles,
Suharto? Shinjuku?

Here, at the shore of this once lake of fire, newts return. Eaten
down to earth spirit, dirt's dark hello fits our pardon: "Fear not
one who has practised ten thousand kicks once, but one who
has practised one kick ten thousand times."

Never
again
will unfroth
the nagging difference.

ACKNOWLEDGEMENTS

Kudos to the literary magazine editors of *FreeFall*, *Vallum*, *The Prairie Journal*, and *Descant*, for publishing some of these poems in slightly different form.

Sections of this book were written with the kind support of the Alberta Foundation for the Arts – kisses.

Thanks to my deep, quirky, courageous ones, who over the years have kept me sane – Sarah X. Murphy, Tobias Fürstenhaupt, Sharron Proulx-Turner, Bill Cicon, Roberta Rees, David Eso, Stuart Ian McKay, Sharon Butala, Matt Smith, Richard Harrison, Cecelia and John Frey, Micheline Maylor, David Martin, Vivian Hansen, Kirk Miles, Selina Clary, Jamal Ali, Joan Crate, Rose and David Scollard, Sheri-D Wilson, Bruce Hunter, Adrienne Adams, Kirk Ramdath, Erin Dingle, Paul Zits, Christa Mayer, Marc Lynch, Natalie Simpson, Nikki Sheppy, Karin Moen – group hug!

All my editors past and present, and friends at Talonbooks: Spencer Williams, Shazia Hafiz Ramji, Ann-Marie Metten, Catriona Strang, Greg Gibson, Les Smith, Kevin Williams.

My pulse – June, Janine, Stephanie.

To the Treaty 7 First Nation peoples whose custodianship and loving wisdom for these unceded lands we squat on will teach all and leave none out.

SELECTED SOURCES

Ariel Glucklich, *Sacred Pain: Hurting the Body for the Sake of the Soul*, Oxford University Press, 2001.

Mary Wollstonecraft Shelley, *Frankenstein; or, The Modern Prometheus*, Lackington, Hughes, Harding, Mavor & Jones, 1818.

John Milton, *Paradise Lost*, Samuel Simmons, 1667; reprinted The Odyssey Press, 1957.

Gertrude Stein, *Bee Time Vine and Other Pieces, 1913–1927*, Yale University Press, 1953.

Rosemary Sadlier, *Harriet Tubman: Freedom Seeker, Freedom Leader*, Dundurn Press, 2012.

Bruce Lee, *Letters of the Dragon: An Anthology of Bruce Lee's Correspondence with Family, Friends, and Fans, 1958–1973*, edited by John Little, Charles E. Tuttle Co., 1998.

Weyman Chan's second book, *Noise from the Laundry*, was a finalist for the 2008 Governor General's Literary Award for Poetry and the Acorn-Plantos Award for People's Poetry. He lives in Calgary.